Anna M. Perry

The story of Easter as told in the Book

Anna M. Perry

The story of Easter as told in the Book

ISBN/EAN: 9783741117886

Manufactured in Europe, USA, Canada, Australia, Japa

Cover: Foto ©Lupo / pixelio.de

Manufactured and distributed by brebook publishing software
(www.brebook.com)

Anna M. Perry

The story of Easter as told in the Book

The Story of Easter

AS TOLD IN THE BOOK.

New York:

ANSON D. F. RANDOLPH & COMPANY.

✠

*THIS narrative of the Resurrection and As-
cension is taken from a volume entitled "The
Life of our Lord, in the Words of the Four
Evangelists. Being the Four Gospels arranged
in Chronological Order, and interwoven to form
a Continuous Narrative." In this reprint of the
closing chapters, the text has been put into para-
graphs, instead of the ordinary form of chapter
and verse.*

✠

✠

Suffered under Pontius Pilate; Was crucified, dead, and buried; He descended into Hell; The third day He rose from the dead; He ascended into Heaven, and sitteth on the right hand of God the Father Almighty; From thence He shall come to judge the quick and the dead.

✠

The Story of Easter.

————✠————

ND, behold, *there was* a rich man of Arimathea, a city of the Jews, named Joseph, an honorable counsellor, a good and just man; (The same had not consented to the counsel and deed of them) who also himself waited for the kingdom of God. And now when the even was come, because it was the preparation, that is, the day before the Sabbath, this *man*, being a disciple of Jesus, but secretly for fear of the Jews, came, and went in boldly unto Pilate, and craved the body of Jesus. And Pilate marvelled if He were already dead: and calling *unto him* the centurion, he asked him whether He had been any while dead. And when he knew *it* of the centurion, he commanded the body to be delivered to Joseph.

Joseph therefore bought fine linen, and took down the body of Jesus, and wrapped it in a

clean linen cloth; And there came also Nicodemus, (which at the first came to Jesus by night,) and brought a mixture of myrrh and aloes, about a hundred pound *weight.* Then took they the body of Jesus, and wound it in linen clothes with the spices, as the manner of the Jews is to bury. Now in the place where He was crucified, there was a garden; and in the garden a new sepulchre, [Joseph's] own new tomb, which he had hewn out in the rock; wherein never man before was laid. There laid they Jesus, therefore because of the Jews' preparation *day;* for the sepulchre was nigh at hand. And [they] rolled a great stone to the door of the sepulchre, and departed. And the women also, Mary Magdalene, and the other Mary, *the mother* of Joses, which came with Him from Galilee, followed after, and sitting over against the sepulchre, beheld the sepulchre, and how His body was laid. And that day was the preparation, and the Sabbath drew on. And they returned, and prepared spices and ointments; and rested the Sabbath day according to the commandment.

Now the next day, that followed the day of the preparation, the chief priests and Pharisees came together unto Pilate saying,

6

Sir, we remember that that deceiver said, while He was yet alive, After three days I will rise again. Command therefore that the sepulchre be made sure until the third day, lest His disciples come by night, and steal Him away, and say unto the people, He is risen from the dead: so the last error shall be worse than the first.

Pilate said unto them,

Ye have a watch: go your way, make *it* as sure as ye can.

So they went, and made the sepulchre sure, sealing the stone, and setting a watch.

And when the sabbath was past, Mary Magdalene, and Mary the *mother* of James, and Salome, bought sweet spices, that they might come and anoint Him. And as it began to dawn toward the first *day* of the week, behold there was a great earthquake: for the angel of the Lord descended from heaven, and came and rolled back the stone from the door, and sat upon it. His countenance was like lightning, and his raiment white as snow: and for fear of him the keepers did shake, and became as dead *men*. And many bodies of the saints which slept, arose, and came out of the graves after [the] resurrection,

7

and went into the holy city, and appeared unto many.

And very early in the morning, when it was yet dark, came Mary Magdalene and the other Mary to the sepulchre, bringing the spices which they had prepared, and certain *other* [women] with them. And they said among themselves,

Who shall roll us away the stone from the door of the sepulchre?

And when they looked, they saw that the stone was rolled away: for it was very great. Then runneth [Mary Magdalene] and cometh to Simon Peter, and to the other disciple, whom Jesus loved, and saith unto them,

They have taken away the Lord out of the sepulchre, and we know not where they have laid Him!

[But the other women] entered into the sepulchre, and saw a young man sitting on the right side, clothed in a long white garment; and they were affrighted. And the angel answered and said unto the women,

Fear not ye: for I know that ye seek Jesus of Nazareth, which was crucified: He is not here: for He is risen, as He said! Behold the place where they laid Him. And go quickly,

8

and tell His disciples and Peter, that He is risen from the dead; and, behold, He goeth before you into Galilee as He said unto you; there shall ye see Him: lo, I have told you!

And they went out quickly, and fled from the sepulchre; for they trembled and were amazed. And behold, two men stood by them in shining garments. And as they were afraid, and bowed down *their* faces to the earth, they said unto them,

Why seek ye the living among the dead? He is not here, but is risen! Remember how He spake unto you when He was yet in Galilee, saying, The Son of man must be delivered into the hands of sinful men, and be crucified, and the third day rise again.

And they remembered His words, and departed quickly from the sepulchre with fear and great joy; neither said they anything to any *man*, for they were afraid, but did run to bring His disciples word.

Now when they were going, behold, some of the watch came into the city, and shewed unto the chief priests all the things that were done. And when they were assembled with the elders, and had taken counsel, they gave large money unto the soldiers, saying,

Say ye, His disciples came by night, and stole Him *away* while we slept. And if this come to the governor's ears, we will persuade him, and secure you.

So they took the money, and did as they were taught: and this saying is commonly reported among the Jews until this day.

[Now when Mary Magdalene came] to Simon Peter, and to the other disciple, whom Jesus loved, and saith unto them,

They have taken away the Lord out of the sepulchre, and we know not where they have laid Him, then arose Peter, and went forth, and that other disciple, and came to the sepulchre.

So they ran both together: and the other disciple did outrun Peter, and came first to the sepulchre. And he stooping down, *and looking in*, saw the linen clothes lying; yet went he not in. Then cometh Simon Peter following him, and went into the sepulchre, and seeth the linen clothes laid by themselves; And the napkin that was about His head, not lying with the linen clothes, but wrapped together in a place by itself. Then went in also that other disciple, which came first to the sepulchre, and he saw, and believed. For as

10

yet they knew not the Scripture, that He must rise again from the dead. Then the disciples went away again unto their own home, wondering at that which was come to pass.

But Mary stood without at the sepulchre weeping: and as she wept, she stooped down *and looked* into the sepulchre, and seeth two angels in white sitting, the one at the head, and the other at the feet, where the body of Jesus had lain. And they say unto her,

Woman, why weepest thou?

She saith unto them,

Because they have taken away my Lord, and I know not where they have laid Him.

And when she had thus said, she turned herself back, and saw Jesus standing, and knew not that it was Jesus. Jesus saith unto her,

Woman, why weepest thou? whom seekest thou?

She supposing Him to be the gardener, saith unto Him,

Sir, if thou have borne Him hence, tell me where thou hast laid Him, and I will take Him away.

Jesus saith unto her,

Mary!

She turned herself, and saith unto Him,

Rabboni! which is to say, Master!

Jesus saith unto her,

Touch me not; for I am not yet ascended to My Father: but go to My brethren, and say unto them, I ascend unto My Father, and your Father; and *to* My God, and your God.

Mary Magdalene came and told the disciples that she had seen the Lord, and *that* He had spoken these things unto her.

✠   ✠   ✠

NOW when *Jesus* was risen early the first *day* of the week, He appeared first to Mary Magdalene, out of whom He had cast seven devils. *And* she went and told them that had been with Him, as they mourned and wept. And they, when they had heard that He was alive, and had been seen of her, believed not.

And as Joanna, and Mary *the mother* of James, and the other *women that were* with them, went to tell His disciples [that He was risen from the dead], behold, Jesus met them, saying,

All hail!

And they came and held Him by the feet, and worshipped Him. Then said Jesus unto them,

Be not afraid: go tell My brethren that they go into Galilee, and there shall they see Me.

And they went and told all these things unto the eleven, and to all the rest; and their words seemed to them as idle tales, and they believed them not.

After that He appeared in another form unto two of them, that same day, as they walked into the country to a village called Emmaus, which was from Jerusalem *about* threescore furlongs. And they talked together of all these things which had happened. And it came to pass, that, while they communed *together* and reasoned, Jesus Himself drew near, and went with them. But their eyes were holden that they should not know Him.

And He said unto them, What manner of communications *are* these that ye have one to another, as ye walk, and are sad?

And the one of them, whose name was Cleopas, answering said unto Him,

Art Thou only a stranger in Jerusalem, and hast not known the things which are come to pass there in these days?

13

And He said unto them,

What things?

And they said unto Him,

Concerning Jesus of Nazareth, which was a prophet mighty in deed and word before God and all the people: and how the chief priests and our rulers delivered Him to be condemned to death, and have crucified Him. But we trusted that it had been He which should have redeemed Israel: and beside all this, to-day is the third day since these things were done.

Yea, and certain women also of our company made us astonished, which were early at the sepulchre; And when they found not His body, they came, saying, that they had also seen a vision of angels, which said that He was alive. And certain of them which were with us, went to the sepulchre, and found *it* even so as the women had said: but Him they saw not.

Then He said unto them,

O fools, and slow of heart to believe all that the prophets have spoken! Ought not Christ to have suffered these things, and to enter into His glory?

And beginning at Moses and all the prophets, He expounded unto them in all the Scriptures, the things concerning Himself.

And they drew nigh unto the village, whither they went: and He made as though He would have gone further: but they constrained Him, saying,

Abide with us; for it is toward evening, and the day is far spent.

And he went in to tarry with them.

And it came to pass, as He sat at meat with them, He took bread, and blessed *it*, and brake, and gave to them. And their eyes were opened, and they knew Him; and He vanished out of their sight.

And they said one to another,

Did not our heart burn within us, while He talked with us by the way, and while He opened to us the Scriptures?

And they rose up the same hour, and returned to Jerusalem the same day at evening, (being the first *day* of the week,) and found the [disciples] gathered together at meat, and them that were with them, saying,

The Lord is risen indeed, and hath appeared to Simon.

And they told what things *were done* in the way, and how He was known of them in

breaking of bread. And as they thus spake, [and] when the doors were shut where the disciples were assembled, for fear of the Jews, Jesus Himself stood in the midst of them, and saith unto them,

Peace *be* unto you.

But they were terrified and affrighted, and supposed that they had seen a spirit. And He said unto them,

Why are ye troubled? and why do thoughts arise in your hearts? Behold My hands and My feet, that it is I Myself: handle Me, and see; for a spirit hath not flesh and bones, as ye see Me have.

And when He had thus spoken, He shewed them *His* hands and feet, and His side. Then were the disciples glad, when they saw the Lord. And while they yet believed not for joy, and wondered, He said unto them,

Have ye here any meat?

And they gave Him a piece of a broiled fish, and of an honeycomb: and He took *it*, and did eat before them. And He upbraided them with their unbelief and hardness of heart, because they believed not them which had seen Him after He was risen. And He said unto them,

These *are* the words which I spake unto

you, while I was yet with you, that all things must be fulfilled, which were written in the law of Moses, and *in* the prophets, and *in* the psalms, concerning Me.

Then opened He their understanding, that they might understand the Scriptures, And said unto them,

Thus it is written, and thus it behoved Christ to suffer, and to rise from the dead the third day: And that repentance and remission of sins should be preached in His name among all nations, beginning at Jerusalem. And ye are witnesses of these things.

And He said unto them,

Go ye into all the world, and preach the gospel to every creature. He that believeth and is baptized, shall be saved; but he that believeth not, shall be damned. And these signs shall follow them that believe; In My name shall they cast out devils; they shall speak with new tongues; they shall take up serpents; and if they drink any deadly thing, it shall not hurt them; they shall lay hands on the sick, and they shall recover.

Then said Jesus to them again,

Peace *be* unto you: as *My* Father hath sent Me, even so send I you.

And when He had said this He breathed on *them*, and saith unto them,

Receive ye the Holy Ghost. Whosesoever sins ye remit, they are remitted unto them; *and* whosesoever *sins* ye retain, they are retained.

But Thomas, one of the twelve, called Didymus, was not with them when Jesus came. The other disciples therefore said unto him,

We have seen the Lord!

But he said unto them,

Except I shall see in His hands the print of the nails, and put my finger into the print of the nails, and thrust my hand into His side, I will not believe.

And after eight days, again His disciples were within, and Thomas with them: *then* came Jesus, the doors being shut, and stood in the midst, and said,

Peace *be* unto you.

Then saith He to Thomas,

Reach hither thy finger, and behold My hands; and reach hither thy hand, and thrust *it* into My side; and be not faithless, but believing.

And Thomas answered and said unto Him,
My Lord and my God.
Jesus saith unto him,
Thomas, because thou hast seen Me, thou hast believed: blessed *are* they that have not seen, and *yet* have believed.

✠ ✠ ✠

AFTER these things Jesus shewed Himself again to the disciples at the sea of Tiberias; and on this wise shewed He *Himself*. There were together Simon Peter, and Thomas called Didymus, and Nathanael of Cana in Galilee, and the *sons* of Zebedee, and two other of His disciples. Simon Peter saith unto them,
I go a fishing.
They say unto him,
We also go with thee.
They went forth, and entered into a ship immediately; and that night they caught nothing. But when the morning was now come, Jesus stood on the shore; but the disciples knew not that it was Jesus. Then Jesus saith unto them,

Children, have ye any meat?
They answered Him,
No.
And He said unto them,
Cast the net on the right side of the ship,
and ye shall find.

They cast therefore, and now they were not
able to draw it for the multitude of fishes.
Therefore that disciple whom Jesus loved, saith
unto Peter,

It is the Lord!

Now when Simon Peter heard that it was
the Lord, he girt *his* fisher's coat *unto him*,
(for he was naked,) and did cast himself into
the sea. And the other disciples came in a
little ship, (for they were not far from land,
but as it were two hundred cubits,) dragging
the net with fishes. As soon then as they
were come to land, they saw a fire of coals
there, and fish laid thereon, and bread.

Jesus saith unto them,

Bring of the fish which ye have now
caught.

Simon Peter went up, and drew the net to
land full of great fishes, an hundred and fifty
and three: and for all there were so many, yet
was not the net broken.

Jesus saith unto them,

Come *and* dine.

And none of the disciples durst ask Him, Who art Thou? knowing that it was the Lord. Jesus then cometh, and taketh bread, and giveth them, and fish likewise. This is now the third time that Jesus shewed Himself to His disciples, after that He was risen from the dead.

So when they had dined, Jesus saith to Simon Peter,

Simon, *son* of Jonas, lovest thou Me more than these?

He saith unto Him,

Yea, Lord; Thou knowest that I love Thee.

He saith unto him,

Feed My lambs.

He saith to him again the second time,

Simon, *son* of Jonas, lovest thou Me?

He saith unto Him,

Yea, Lord; Thou knowest that I love Thee.

He saith unto him,

Feed My sheep.

He saith unto him the third time,

Simon, *son* of Jonas, lovest thou Me?

Peter was grieved because He said unto

him the third time, Lovest thou Me? And he said unto Him,

Lord, Thou knowest all things; Thou knowest that I love Thee.

Jesus saith unto him,

Feed My sheep.

Verily, verily, I say unto thee, When thou wast young, thou girdedst thyself, and walkedst whither thou wouldest: but when thou shalt be old, thou shalt stretch forth thy hands, and another shall gird thee, and carry *thee* whither thou wouldest not.

This spake He, signifying by what death he should glorify God. And when He had spoken this, He saith unto him,

Follow Me.

Then Peter, turning about, seeth the disciple whom Jesus loved, following; which also leaned on His breast at supper, and said,

Lord, which is he that betrayeth Thee?

Peter seeing him, saith to Jesus,

Lord, and what *shall* this man *do?*

Jesus saith unto him,

If I will that he tarry till I come, what *is that* to thee? follow thou Me.

Then went this saying abroad among the brethren, that that disciple should not die: yet

Jesus said not unto him, He shall not die; but, If I will that he tarry till I come, what *is that* to thee?

This is the disciple which testifieth of these things, and wrote these things : and we know that his testimony is true.

After that, the eleven disciples went away into Galilee, into a mountain where Jesus had appointed them : [and] He was seen of above five hundred brethren at once; of whom the greater part remain unto this present, but some are fallen asleep. And when they saw Him, they worshipped Him: but some doubted. And Jesus came and spake unto them, saying,

All power is given unto Me in heaven and in earth. Go ye therefore, and teach all nations, baptizing them in the name of the Father, and of the Son, and of the Holy Ghost: Teaching them to observe all things whatsoever I have commanded you: and, lo, I am with you alway, *even* unto the end of the world.

After that, He was seen of James; then of all the apostles; to whom also He shewed Himself alive after His passion by many infal-

lible proofs, being seen of them forty days, and speaking of the things pertaining to the kingdom of God : And, being assembled together with *them*, commanded them that they should not depart from Jerusalem, but wait for the promise of the Father, which, *saith He*, ye have heard of Me.

For John truly baptized with water ; but ye shall be baptized with the Holy Ghost not many days hence.

When they therefore were come together [at Jerusalem], they asked of Him, saying,

Lord, wilt Thou at this time restore again the kingdom to Israel ?

And He said unto them, It is not for you to know the times or the seasons, which the Father hath put in His own power. But ye shall receive power, after that the Holy Ghost is come upon you : and ye shall be witnesses unto Me both in Jerusalem, and in all Judea, and in Samaria, and unto the uttermost part of the earth. And, behold, I send the promise of My Father upon you : but tarry ye in the city of Jerusalem, until ye be endued with power from on high.

So then, after the Lord had spoken these things unto them, He led them out as far as

24

to Bethany, unto the mount called Olivet, which is from Jerusalem a sabbath day's journey, and He lifted up His hands, and blessed them. And it came to pass, while He blessed them, He was parted from them, and, while they beheld, He was taken up into heaven, and a cloud received Him out of their sight. And while they looked steadfastly toward heaven as He went up, behold, two men stood by them in white apparel; Which also said,

Ye men of Galilee, why stand ye gazing up into heaven? this same Jesus, which is taken up from you into heaven, shall so come in like manner as ye have seen Him go into heaven.

Then they worshipped Him, and returned to Jerusalem with great joy; And were continually in the temple, praising and blessing God.

✠   ✠   ✠

ND many other signs truly did Jesus in the presence of His disciples, which are not written in this book: But these are written, that ye might believe that Jesus is the Christ, the Son of God; and that believing, ye might have life through His name. And [the disciples] went forth, and preached everywhere, the Lord working with *them*, and confirming the word with signs following.

.

www.ingramcontent.com/pod-product-compliance
Lightning Source LLC
Chambersburg PA
CBHW031818090426

42739CB00008B/1321